To my uncle Les

God bless you

Joan Cochran

EVERYDAY CHOICES
MONUMENTAL
OUTCOMES

8 Daily Decisions You Can Make to Change Your Life

BY LOREN CARLSON

Published by Loren Carlson

Cover Design and Content Layout By:
Elvie Communications and Design
Elviedesigns1@gmail.com

Library of Congress Cataloging-in-Publication Data

ISBN: 978-1723520341, 723520349

Library of Congress Control Number: 2018958020

Printed in the United States of America

Les, I told Glady I had written a book and I've sent her a copy, I got your address from her to send you one as well. It's available on Amazon so far and I've sold a few copies. Amazing! I hear you are doing pretty good, glad to hear that. Well I'll send this along and maybe you can get some enjoyment out of it. God bless, Loren

DEDICATION

To Cheryl, my wife of 47 years: Your dedication to the Lord, commitment to truth and faithfulness to me is something special. Thank you for sticking with me all these years. I'm looking forward to what God will continue to do through us for His kingdom.

PRAISE FOR EVERYDAY DECISIONS MONUMENTAL OUTCOMES

I have known Pastor Loren and Cheryl Carlson for several years. I have appreciated their Godly character and steady walk of faith. *Everyday Decisions Monumental Outcomes* is written to help you live a victorious life.

We are defined by our choices. Most people tend to abdicate their responsibilities in following the Lord. This book helps you to hear the voice of God and to follow the practical leadings of the Holy Spirit. The nuggets that you pull from this book will give stability to your life. I highly recommend this book to you.

Pastor Dave Kaufman
Holy Life Tabernacle, Brookings, SD

CONTENTS

FOREWORD

I love this subject - making right choices - because our daily choices can make a monumental difference in our lives. My good friend Loren Carlson has penned a masterpiece on the purest form of the gospel. He presents to us eight major choices we face in this life. As we choose the path that God has set before us, we can experience life to the fullest and experience the quality and abundance that God has intended for each of us, and avoid detours and disasters.

This simple yet profound book explains the gospel with exceptional clarity. Life's choices don't have to be complicated. If we are not dominated by our own self will but look for help and guidance of the Holy Spirit, He promises to order our steps. We are not alone and the Helper will let us see things from His perspective.

God wants each of us to experience abundant life - life to the full. He is not against us, but to the contrary, is committed to helping us walk in a path that will bring fulfillment beyond our wildest expectations.

Steve Sampson
Conference Speaker and Author

INTRODUCTION

I've heard there is a point along the Continental Divide high in the Rocky Mountains in Colorado at which the waters of a small stream separate. It would not seem to matter much whether a drop of water goes to the left or to the right, but the outcome of those drops of water is totally different. One drop goes to the west and eventually flows into the Colorado River and empties into the Gulf of California and the Pacific Ocean. Another drop goes east until it flows into the Mississippi River and dumps into the Gulf of Mexico and the Atlantic Ocean. Two tiny drops of water, but one small turning point, determines the outcome of two entirely different destinations.

Many choices in life are like that, at the time they seem insignificant. Yet those choices may set in motion a series of events which shape our life and the lives of our children and grandchildren after us.

During the summer of my junior year in high school, my family moved to another school district. At the beginning of the school year I was getting used to the new system and playing sports, so I didn't try out for the upcoming school play. One day the director asked me if I would consider being the lead in the play because the kid who was going to play that part quit. Not thinking much of it and full of youthful cockiness, I decided to do it. I was playing a husband and the prettiest girl in school was playing my wife. Well, sparks flew and now I've been married to that pretty girl for 47 years.

That choice worked out great for me, but sometimes people make unwise choices which aren't momentous in themselves, but they lead to tragedies: choosing to ride with a friend who has been drinking, resulting in a serious accident and death; a business executive with financial problems put in charge of large amounts of money makes the choice to siphon some for himself and ends up in prison.

Each of us is faced with choices every single day of our lives that can lead to vastly different outcomes. Do you forgive when a loved one hurts you or hold a grudge? Do you look away from pornography or lust when it presents itself or indulge? Are you a faithful employee, or do you try to get by doing as little as possible when the boss isn't looking? When someone talks badly about you do you lash out at them or offer grace? These daily choices we make can have a major impact on our life and the life of those we love.

When the Apollo space program was sending rockets to the moon in the 1960s, they didn't simply launch a rocket from Houston and hope to hit the moon. They had to make course corrections every 10 minutes or so for the entire three day trip and even then, they only landed a few feet inside the 500 mile target zone. It is the same with us. All of our life we must make wise, daily course corrections so that we can "hit the mark" of making good choices that produce monumental outcomes.

God has provided in His word everything we have need of to help us make these day-to-day course corrections that bring life to us and everyone we come in contact with. In the pages that follow, you will discover eight choices based on scripture that will pave the way for positive outcomes in your life. "The wise will hear and increase their learning, and the person of under-standing will acquire wise counsel *and* the skill [to steer his course wisely and lead others to the truth]" (Prov. 1:5).

CHOICE # 1
Choose to Believe God

This choice to believe God or not, without doubt, is the most important one that every person on the planet will make. Look at what the writer of Proverbs had to say about the benefit of believing and trusting in the Lord:

> Trust in and rely confidently on the LORD with all your heart and do not rely on your own insight or understanding. In all your ways know and acknowledge and recognize Him, and He will make your paths

straight and smooth [removing obstacles that block your way] (Prov. 3:5-6).

Perhaps you have noticed that God seems to always have promises associated with His "suggestions." If we trust and rely on Him, His insights, His wisdom, and His knowledge, He will direct us to paths that are straight and move obstacles out of the way. It's hard to imagine anyone not wanting to know what paths to take in life and perhaps more importantly, how to choose those paths. I wonder if you've ever thought of the fact that God clearly has a vantage point when it comes to our life. It makes perfect sense to trust Him and the directives that are found in His infallible Word.

With Adam and Eve, a run in with a snake had a monumental outcome. As we ponder that story it seems that this would be a no-brainer of a choice; believe what God had told them or believe the deceiver. But as we know, out of that choice came a monumental outcome, not just for them but for the whole world. Eve was convinced by a talking snake that she didn't have everything she needed to make her happy. Have you ever asked yourself, "how could this happen?" It's understandable how people in today's world are discontented and looking for something, but Adam and Eve were perfect, living in a perfect world with no problems. How could they fall for such a line?

Perhaps one of the factors in this poor choice was that Adam and Eve didn't really know God. What?!??!? They walked and talked with God every day, they lived in

God clearly has a vantage point when it comes to our life.

His Garden, they were a product of the original creation. Of course they knew God! But think about it. They didn't really know the nature and character of a loving God, even in this perfect environment, or they would never have believed the lie that God was keeping something good from them. God gave Adam and Eve a free will to believe or not to believe. Before Satan could tempt Eve to eat the forbidden fruit, he had to make her believe that the Lord didn't have her best interests in mind.

> "But the serpent said to the woman, 'You certainly will not die! For God knows that on the day you eat from it your eyes will be opened [that is, you will have greater awareness], and you will be like God, knowing [the difference between] good and evil'" (Gen. 3:4–5).

Satan says, "See, Eve, God is keeping you from being like Him, but if you eat of this beautiful tree, you can know the difference between good and evil. God is keeping things from you; that's why He doesn't want you to eat of the tree." Just a simple, everyday choice, right? Eat some fruit or don't eat some fruit, what could come of that? Adam and Eve had been given everything, but they became convinced that they hadn't. And the enemy's tactics have not changed. Every sin, every decision we make to disobey God and do our own thing, is because we really don't believe that God has provided everything we need for this life.

Humanly speaking, how did Adam and Eve know there wasn't something better out there? They didn't know what bad was, they had no way to compare how good God was, so they bought into the lie.

> "And when the woman saw that the tree was good for food, and that it was delightful to look at, and a tree to be desired in order to make one wise and insightful, she took some of its fruit and ate it; and she also gave some to her husband with her, and he ate" (Gen. 3:6).

Adam and Eve chose to believe the lies of the devil rather than the Word from God because they didn't understand the nature of His heart. It is imperative that we come to know for ourselves the nature, character and love of God so that we can trust and believe in Him when His Word offers to direct our steps. Here's Paul's prayer for that exact thing:

> "For this reason I kneel before the Father from whom every family in heaven and on earth is named. I pray that he may grant you, according to the riches of his glory, to be strengthened with power in your inner being through his Spirit, and that Christ may dwell in your hearts through faith. I pray that you, being rooted and firmly established in love, may be able to comprehend with all the saints what is the length and width, height and depth of God's love, and to know Christ's love that surpasses knowledge, so that you may be filled with all the fullness of God" (Eph. 3:14–19).

So how do we know that God and His Word can be trusted so we can believe and not doubt? This passage tells us how. We come to know for ourselves His great love. When

Keeping God's commands is a result of knowing God.

you love someone, what do you do for them? You provide for them, you encourage them, you make sure they are taken care of in every way, and I think it is safe to say you would never lie to them. God says He is not a man that He can lie. If He promises something in His Word He is obligated to back it up and bring it to pass when we believe and declare it.

In John 5:19 Jesus said, "the Son can do nothing by himself; he can do only what he sees his Father doing, because whatever the Father does the Son also does." Jesus existed from the beginning and He perfectly reflected God's will, nature, and character while He was on earth. Since Jesus is the Word become flesh, and He and God are in agreement in everything, God and His Word can be trusted to navigate us through life.

Here are additional assurances God gives us that His Word can be trusted: "My covenant will I not break, nor alter the thing that is gone out of My lips" (Psalm 89:34). "He keeps his word even to his own disadvantage and does not change it [for his own benefit]" (Psalm 15:4b)

God will put a Yes! and Amen! to His Word even to His own hurt. He never changes His mind or goes back on what His Word says. If we come to know for ourselves the nature and heart and love of God and believe that the Truth of His Word was solidified in the sinless life, death, resurrection and ascension of Jesus His Son, then we can trust His Word and believe God to take care of us and give us everything we need no matter what we have to go through in life.

Another issue that arises when it comes to believing and trusting in God and His Word is rightly dividing the Word of Truth. If you know the nature and heart of God then you look at His Word in that light. But if you think that God is a tyrant or is a hard God, or that His Word is always for correction and punishment you look at it differently. The author of the book of I John says this,

> "This is how we know that we know him: if we keep his commands. The one who says, "I have come to know him," and yet doesn't keep his commands, is a liar, and the truth is not in him. But whoever keeps his word, truly in him the love of God is

made complete. This is how we know we are in him" (2:3-5).

A spiritually dyslexic person looks at these verses and says, "I want to know God, so I must keep His commands," when in actuality these verses are saying just the opposite. Keeping God's commands is a *result* of knowing God. In fact, seeking to know the Lord better by living a holier life is opposite of what 1 John 2 is saying. In Paul's prayer for those in Ephesus, he instructs the believers that when God's love is perfected in us, keeping God's Word will be the result.

Any attempt to reverse this order will not work and yet that is what many are doing. This confusion has caused many to tie God's love for them to their performance. So many people try to live a holy and religious life hoping to get closer to God. But living a holy life will not cause you to experience the length, width, height and depth of the love of God and cause you to trust God and His Word.

On the contrary, trusting God and His Word because you have experienced the length, width, height and depth of His love will cause you to live a holy life. This knowledge will also give you the insights you need to make positive, every day choices that bring about great outcomes. One of the most important choices you will ever make is to truly know and believe God and His Word.

CHOICE # 2
Choose to Forget the Past

Here's what Paul had to say about his past:

I do not consider, brethren, that I have captured and made it my own [yet]; but one thing I do [it is my one aspiration]: forgetting what lies behind and straining forward to what lies ahead, I press on toward the goal to win the [supreme and heavenly] prize to which God in Christ Jesus is calling us upward (Phil. 3:13).

The word "forgetting" in the Greek is *epilanthanomai*, and it means "to forget...given over to oblivion" (Thayer's Greek-English Lexicon). The Greek verb for "straining forward" is *epekteinomai,* and it means "to stretch out" and "to stretch (oneself) forward to" (Thayer's Greek-English Lexicon). Paul is using the analogy of a runner that is running in the Greek games for the prize.

Most in the church world would probably agree that Paul was one of the most successful Christians who ever lived. In this passage, he gave us one of his secrets of spiritual success: Paul's heart was not divided. He was committed to what lies ahead and not behind, to win the prize of eternal life.

In our modern world, the laser is an important tool. It is used to shrink or destroy tumors, polyps, or precancerous growths. It relieves symptoms of cancer, removes kidney stones, improves vision, cauterizes blood vessels to help prevent blood loss, and a myriad of other things. Ordinary white light is a combination of different wavelengths or colors. The laser, however, is concentrated light of one, monochromatic wavelength (color) that can accomplish amazing results.

Singleness of purpose and vision, one wavelength, is an absolute necessity to victorious Christian living and conversely is important in our decision making as well. If we are focused on our past, our mistakes, failures and shortcomings, it's extremely difficult to move forward with our life or even make productive choices because we are running them through the filter of our past instead of the truth of God's Word.

But Jesus said to him, "No one who puts his hand to the plow and looks back [to the things left behind] is fit for the kingdom of God" (Luke 9:62). In the farming community if we are using a piece of tillage equipment to turn the soil, and only focus on where we've been, we will be driving all over the field because we aren't looking where we are going. The enemy of our soul is really good at trying to make us do the same thing. Have you noticed the devil's tactic is to bring up your past because there is nothing you can do to change it? It is easy to get us into guilt and condemnation over past failures because we are powerless to alter an outcome that has already happened. If we are constantly looking back at our past in regret and shame, it severely limits our ability to remain laser focused on the path ahead.

Paul had a past - a past that I'm sure he could have regretted had he spent time pondering it. But he says in Philippians chapter three that he was forgetting that part of his life and pressing forward to what God had for him (v. 13). Some people have misunderstood this passage and taught that we are to forget everything in the past. That is not what Paul was saying. The Scriptures teach us that

> **Singleness of purpose and vision is an absolute necessity to victorious decision making.**

memory can be a very powerful force for good in our lives. There are accounts in the Bible where God would remind the Israelites what He had done for their forefathers so they would have confidence He would do it for them. But in Philippians 3, Paul is speaking about forgetting all the things that he used to trust in prior to his salvation experience. Here is a sampling from verses four through eight:

> I once also had confidence in the flesh. If anyone else thinks he has grounds for confidence in the flesh, I have more: circumcised the eighth day; of the nation of Israel, of the tribe of Benjamin, a Hebrew born of Hebrews; regarding the law, a

Pharisee regarding zeal, persecuting the church; regarding the righteousness that is in the law, blameless. But everything that was a gain to me, I have considered to be a loss because of Christ. More than that, I also consider everything to be a loss in view of the surpassing value of knowing Christ Jesus my Lord. Because of Him I have suffered the loss of all things and consider them filth, so that I may gain Christ.

In other translations, Paul uses the word dung or manure to explain the worth of past accomplishments because those things he once took pride in offered no means of providing his salvation or gave him any spiritual benefit. Paul "forgot," ceased to depend on, his own accomplishments and accolades and focused only on what Christ had done for him. Our faults and failures, those things that make us look back upon our life in shame, guilt or regret, must be "forgotten" in comparison to the forgiveness and restoration we have in Christ Jesus. Also those things we have accomplished in our own strength and abilities, that we once trusted as a source of pride, must be set aside in comparison to the wonderful work that Jesus did on Calvary's cross.

There are things of our past that we can learn so we don't do them again or use to motivate us to do things better. I think of Peter, certainly one of the most dynamic apostles of Christendom, but he wasn't always that way. It seems that when Peter was walking with Je-

> **For time and the world do not stand still. Change is the Law of Life. And those who look only to the past or the present are certain to miss the future.**
> - John F. Kennedy

sus, he often just opened his mouth to "change feet", as the saying goes. He told Jesus that he would not allow Him to go to the cross and Jesus told Satan to get behind Him. He cut off Malchus' ear in trying to protect Jesus and was reprimanded for it. His most egregious sin, however, was emphatically telling those accusing him of being a disciple, that he never knew Jesus and running away in shame.

When Peter was restored to favor on the shore of Galilee, Jesus looked past all of Peter's failures and simply asked him to feed His sheep. From that moment on, Peter never looked back at those failures. He even ended up dying on an upside-down cross. Peter's past failures may have been the catalyst for his successes and faithfulness in his living for Christ, even unto death. Peter remembered that he never wanted to feel the way he felt after he rejected Jesus and set his eyes completely on the work and calling in front of him.

Are there things in your past that have been or could be beneficial in moving you forward in your journey with Jesus? I like to look back over my life from time to time to see if I am learning, if I am growing in the knowledge and wisdom of God. Has my wrong thinking been replaced with godly wisdom and discernment? Have I changed the way I do things so that what used to get me into trouble or guilt and condemnation, has now been replaced with things that are beneficial? I learn from the past but I don't live in it.

Early in my marriage and in my walk with the Lord, I was teaching and coaching at a high school. After five years I was offered a position selling insurance and it looked like a real chance to make some money. An everyday job choice; one that thousands make every day, right? So I made the choice to take the job. But in the course of the next two years I literally went broke, my wife and I lost our house and most of our possessions.

Forced to get some kind of income, I chose to

accept my dad's offer to join him in his agriculture business. That meant leaving a church where we were growing spiritually and where revival was happening. We left our friends and moved back to where we had grown up. By comparison, moving home seemed like a spiritual desert.

Not too many weeks into the move, I was discouraged; wondering if I had made a mistake in moving my family, wondering if God was still with me and whether or not He was aware of my situation. We lived on an acreage at the time, and one night I was out in the yard just crying out to God, "God are You here? God do you still care about me and my family?"

In the middle of this moment of fear and doubt I said, "God if you are still here, if you are still part of all this, let me see a falling star." Instantly realizing that was kind of a foolish thing to put before the Lord, I began to say, "but if you don't I'll still love you." But in that moment, He responded to my cry and like a caring father, gave me what I asked for - a falling star.

Even though I made choices that had caused disruption in my life and the life of my family, God showed me how much He loved me, that He was still with me, and it was going to be okay. I learned

> **I've got my faults, but living in the past is not one of them. There's no future in it.**
> -   Sparky Anderson,
> Major League Baseball coach

from that situation and made a choice that night. I quit regretting the past and I pressed on. Since then I have not doubted His promises. He will never leave or forsake me. He will always be with me and help me. That has made a monumental difference in the way I look at life and the way that I look at God.

That old hymn Amazing Grace, has a phrase in it that is timeless; "I once was lost but now I'm found, was blind but now I see." Forgetting what lies behind and straining forward to what lies ahead, I press on (Phil. 3:13). Forgetting the past things that are detrimental and remembering those things of the past which are beneficial and learning from them, I become a more complete person in Christ. When we make that attitude the basis for choices, the outcomes are beneficial to our life and the lives of those around us.

CHOICE # 3
Choose to Use Your God-Given Authority

Take heed of Luke's words: "Listen carefully: I have given you authority [that you now possess] to tread on serpents and scorpions, and [the ability to exercise authority] over all the power of the enemy (Satan); and nothing will [in any way] harm you" (10:19).

This scripture is speaking of mastery over the spiritual realm of the enemy (Satan). This isn't saying that the enemy of our soul doesn't attempt to bring trials, tribulations and destructions into our life. He does. The Scriptures abound with examples and warnings of the enemy's damage on the godly and the ungodly alike. However, this passage tells us that he cannot harm us when we are walking in faith in Christ's redemptive work; what Jesus has won for us on Calvary's cross.

How do we tread (trample) over all the attacks, temptations and deceptions of the enemy? The Bible says that, "my people perish for lack of knowledge" (Hosea 4:6). If we know who we are in Christ and what power and authority we possess, we will discern when the enemy is attempting to deceive us and reject his advances. That's how we trample on him and his schemes and keep him from harming us.

"Be well balanced and always alert, because your enemy, the devil, roams around incessantly, like a roaring lion looking for its prey to devour. Take a decisive stand against him and resist his every attack with strong, vigorous faith" (1 Peter 5:8-9). The devil roams around looking for someone to devour, in other words, looking for someone who will allow him to devour them. We do that when we allow him to convince us that our past is so terrible God can't help us. We think, "what good does it do to believe God, He's half ticked at us most of the time." We allow him to do that when we fail to use the Word as the weapon of our warfare. The devil has no right to devour us unless we allow it. Just like in the Garden, the devil couldn't take Adam and Eve's authority on the earth from them, he had to deceive them into giving it to him. And that's what the devil tries to do with us, convince us to relinquish our authority to him.

The authority mankind lost in the Garden when Adam and Eve sinned is the very authority Jesus won back for us on Calvary. But the devil's

> **The Truth of God's Word is what removes the deception of the devil and breaks his power over our thinking.**

tactic has not changed. He must deceive us into believing we have no authority against him.

Early in my wife's walk with the Lord she was awakened by a presence in the bedroom. She recognized it as the enemy trying to get her into fear and she asked the Lord to get rid of it. The Lord said, "you tell it to go." Three times she asked Him to get rid of the presence, three times God said, "tell it to go." Finally, after the third time she said, "I command you to leave in the name of Jesus," and the presence immediately left. God was teaching her that she had authority that He had given her to overcome the enemy and his schemes. But she had to make a choice to believe what God was telling her or give in to her fears.

The Bible gives us a look at the difference between God and the enemy of our soul: "The thief (devil) comes only in order to steal and kill

God has given us authority to trample on the attacks of the enemy.

and destroy. I (Jesus) came that they may have *and* enjoy life, and have it in abundance [to the full, till it overflows]" (John 10:10).

I love the clarity of that passage of scripture. The devil may come as an "angel of light" but his only goal is to steal from us, to kill us and destroy us. Anything that is going on in our life that fits into those three categories, isn't from Jesus it's from the enemy.

Jesus wants us to have life; and not only life, but life we can enjoy, and have abundantly, till we are full and overflowing with it. If we understand that basic concept, it will transform our lives. We will cease blaming God for our difficulties and begin resisting the one who is responsible. When the Bible tells us to believe a certain way, or to choose a certain path, we will know and believe it is for our good and overflowing benefit. Hence, better choices, better outcomes.

God has given us authority to trample on the attacks of the enemy, so He isn't going to do it for us.

Therefore our ability to make good choices is greatly enhanced by the knowledge of who we are in Christ Jesus and what the Bible says we possess as weapons of our warfare (2 Cor. 10).

Most of us know the story of David and Goliath. The Israelite army was positioned across from the army of the Philistines. Every day their mighty warrior Goliath -over nine feet tall and what could be called the first recorded tank because of all his armor - would come out and challenge the army of Israel to send out a man to fight him. Whoever would lose would become slaves to the winner. But of course, no one took him up on it.

One day the teenager David was sent by his father to check on his brothers at the camp. During his visit he heard Goliath's challenge. Indignant over this uncircumcised Philistine shaming the army of God, David went to Saul and offered to fight Goliath. Of course, Saul was glad anyone would fight the giant because all of his army was terrified. He offered David his armor and spear, but it was too cumbersome so David headed for the giant with only his sling, a staff, and a few stones from the wadi.

The Philistine came closer and closer to David, with the shield-bearer in front of him. When the Philistine looked and saw David, he despised him because he was just a youth, healthy and handsome. He said to David, 'Am I a dog that you come against me with sticks?' Then he cursed David by his gods. 'Come here,' the Philistine called to David, 'and I'll give your flesh to the birds of the sky and the wild beasts'" (1 Sam. 17:40-44)!

For most, that would be enough to send us packing. This Philistine man had been a warrior from his youth, heavily armored, including an armor bearer going before him. David was all alone. The Israelite army cowered in fear as they watched David head toward what was sure to be his death. Yet out of David's mouth we hear this:

> David said to the Philistine, "You come against me with a sword, spear, and javelin, but I come against you in the name of the LORD of Armies, the God of the ranks of Israel—you have defied him. Today, the LORD will hand you over to me. Today, I'll strike you down, remove your head, and give the corpses of the Philistine camp to the birds of the sky and the wild creatures of the earth. Then all the world will know that Israel has a God, and this whole assembly will know that it is not by

sword or by spear that the LORD saves, for the battle is the LORD's. He will hand you over to us" (1 Sam. 17:45-47).

Notice David said "us." David knew he wasn't alone. David was a young man who had experienced God's protection. He had killed a bear and a lion that had tried to take his sheep and he knew it was God who delivered him from both of them. This Philistine was no different. David wasn't looking at the giant and his armor, he was looking at His God and he knew it was no match. David knew where His strength came from; he stood up to the enemy and his bluster. Outcome? He defeated him.

I want to make another point about this, one that is important in our making wise choices. God gave David a strategy:

> When the Philistine started forward to attack him, David ran quickly to the battle line to meet the Philistine David put his hand in the bag, took out a stone, slung it, and hit the Philistine on his forehead. The stone sank into his forehead, and he fell facedown to the ground. David defeated

the Philistine with a sling and a stone (1
Sam. 17:48-50)

What person in their right mind would run to meet this giant? If David would have danced around looking for an opening, twirling his sling, the giant would have figured that out and protected himself. But David took off running to close the gap and catch the giant by surprise. Before he could figure out what was going on, David buried a rock in his forehead.

God not only tells us who we are in Him, the authority He has given us to stand up to the enemy, but He gives us a strategy to defeat the schemes and wiles of the devil.

"The wise will hear and increase their learning, and the person of understanding will acquire wise counsel *and* the skill [to steer his course wisely and lead others to the truth" (Prov. 1:5). Are we going to allow the enemy to run over us and devour us, destroy us and make life miserable? Will we take a stand? With the authority we already possess, and the knowledge we have of His Word, we will make good choices and be an overcomer.

David drew strength and assurance from his past experiences, remembering that God had delivered him from the lion and bear and he knew God would help him defeat the giant. Much of our freedoms come when we make our choices according to our knowledge of God and according to His Word, which is Truth, for the Bible says that it is Truth that sets us free.

Using the name of Jesus is another weapon of our warfare that we exert over the enemy in our confrontations with him. "For this reason also [because He obeyed and so completely humbled Himself], God has highly exalted Him and bestowed on Him the name which is above every name· so that at the name of Jesus EVERY KNEE SHALL BOW [in submission], of those who are in heaven and on earth and under the earth" (Phil. 2:9-10). The exaltation cited in this passage is a reference to Christ's ascension and glorification at the right hand of the Father. Because of Christ's humility and obedience, God has given Him a name that is above every name, in heaven, on earth, and under the earth (vs. 10). There is no exemption for anyone or anything from coming under the Lordship of Jesus. He is Lord of all. And the amazing thing is He has given us that name to use for our defense against the wiles and schemes of the enemy.

Jesus has not only been exalted above every "being" that has a name, but He is also highly exalted above anything else that can be named. If you can put a name on it, Jesus' name is above it. Sickness, poverty, depression, anger, everything has to bow its knee to the Lordship of Jesus. We have been given that name to use as we traverse this thing called life, which includes making good, godly choices that produce "life."

> **God has given Him a name that is above every name.**

So when we couple Philippians 2:9-10 with Luke 10:19 that we began this chapter with, we have the combination that guarantees our success. It is absolutely essential that we realize that it is the knowledge that God is for us, that His Word is true, and Jesus is the name above all names, that ensures our victory over the enemy and his schemes. We have been given authority over the deceitfulness of the demonic realm, the lies and imaginations which the devil tries to deceive us with, and the ability to make great choices that produce great outcomes.

CHOICE # 4
Choose The Treasures You Store in Your Heart

The choices we make are born out of the treasures that are in our heart. "The good man produces what is good and honorable and moral out of the good treasure [stored] in his heart; and the evil man produces what is wicked and depraved out of the evil [in his heart]; for his mouth speaks from the overflow of his heart" (Luke 6:45).

We see this in action in the Bible story of Lot and Abram. They had both become prosperous and each had much livestock, servants and material goods.

Abram went up from Egypt to the Negev—he, his wife, and all he had, and Lot with him. Abram was very rich in livestock, silver, and gold…Now Lot, who was traveling with Abram, also had flocks, herds, and tents. But the land was unable to support them as long as they stayed together, for they had so many possessions that they could not stay together (Genesis 13:1-6).

The herdsmen of Lot and of Abram were quarreling because there wasn't adequate land to support all their flocks. So Abram gave Lot his choice of where to settle. Lot surveyed the land and decided to move down into the lush Jordan valley. That choice was the beginning of Lot's gradual but steady spiritual decline. First he *looked* toward Sodom (13:10). Then he *moved his tents* near Sodom (13:12). Next we find him *living* in Sodom (14:12). Finally he is *sitting in the gate* of Sodom (19:1); he had become a city official.

As the story unfolds, we read of the fiery destruction of Sodom and all the surrounding area where Lot lost his wife and barely escaped with his own life and two daughters. He ends up hiding in a cave where his daughters make him drunk and commit incest with him. The offspring of that union

> **The choices we make are born out of the treasures that are in our heart.**

were the Moabites and the Ammonites; two of Israel's perennial enemies.

It all began with Lot's choice - out of the desire of his heart - to live near and eventually in Sodom. The treasure Lot had in his heart influenced his choices and eventually became his ruin. As we have been discussing, choices often result in significant, even eternal outcomes.

There is a clear progression in this story. First, both Lot and Abram have increased wealth and material possessions. There is nothing wrong or evil in having wealth, but it's what's in our heart that determines whether wealth controls us or we control wealth. Abraham and Lot's *increased wealth* led to *increased strife* because there simply wasn't enough land for each of them.

The increased strife led to *increased responsibility* for choices. Lot wasn't just deciding for himself. His family and now many servants and their families would be affected by his decision. The increased responsibility for choices led to either *increased wickedness* (in Lot's case, choosing Sodom) or *increased blessing* (in Abram's case, choosing Canaan).

Lot did something many do, even Christians, usually without much thought; He made a major life decision based on the unchallenged assumption that pursuing prosperity should be the main goal. Lot chose Sodom because he saw the lush valley and thought he could prosper there. But that faulty desire led him to make the worst choice of his life.

We're given a clue when Genesis 13:10 says that Lot saw the valley "like the land of Egypt." Lot didn't want any part of the hard life of faith, of living in Canaan. He wanted to live the good life of Egypt. He never seemed to consider the spiritual implications of moving his family to Sodom. "But the men of Sodom were extremely wicked and sinful against the Lord, [unashamed in their open sin before Him]" (Genesis 13:13).What Lot treasured in his heart clouded his wisdom in making the choice to move near Sodom and it had monumental consequences for him and his family.

How often are decisions made to move because the husband or wife is offered a better paying job, but never consider how the move will affect the family spiritually. Just like with Lot and Abram, we can't escape from living near sinners (Canaan was almost as bad as Sodom). But many, like Lot, decide where they're going to live based on material gain, not spiritual benefit. This next passage tells us when the trouble began:

"Then Lot chose for himself all the valley of the Jordan, and he traveled east. So they separated from each other." (Genesis 13:11). Lot chose for himself that day and he and his family paid an awful price. "For what does it benefit a man to gain the whole world [with all its pleasures], and forfeit his soul" (Mark 8:36)?

Since many choices have eternally significant consequences, how do we make good choices? As we have discussed, it is making choices in line with the principles of God. Lot has often been criticized for moving to Sodom, but as I mentioned, both Abram and Lot lived in corrupt cultures. To compare the Canaanites with the Sodomites is like comparing Stalin with Hitler. I've heard it said that the Sodomites rated a 10 on the wickedness scale, and the Canaanites a 9.5. So you have to ask, "Why did Abram remain untainted, but Lot became corrupted?"

"Then Abram broke camp and moved his tent and came and settled by the [grove of the great] terebinths (oak trees) of Mamre [the Amorite], which are in Hebron, and there he built an altar to [honor] the LORD" (Gen. 13:18). We see that Abram had different treasures in his heart. Abram was a worshiper. The first thing he did was to build an altar to the Lord, thanking Him for where He was and what the Lord would do for him where he was.

We don't read of Lot building an altar in Sodom, or that he even desired to honor the Lord. Eventually we see him trade in his tent for a home in Sodom, settle in and blend in with their corruption. He was

> **Out of the treasures of our heart, we decide and we act.**

popular, sitting on their city council. Abram, on the other hand, lived in fellowship with God and became known as the friend of God.

Almost everything in life is a heart issue. Think about it; out of the treasures of our heart, we decide and we act. Jesus was the friend of sinners, but He was never tainted by their sin because He put a premium on fellowship with the Father rather than approval of the world. He was in the world with a clear sense of His mission, to glorify the Father and to seek and to save the lost.

If we want to line up with Abram rather than with Lot, we must put fellowship with God above the approval of the world in all of our choices. In fact, Lot's choice of Sodom was based on what would bring him quick gratification, but he didn't take into account God's promise to Abram about the land. After Lot moved to Sodom, the Lord reaffirmed His promise to Abram and even expanded on it:

> The LORD said to Abram, after Lot had left him, 'Now lift up your eyes and look from the place where you are standing, northward and southward and eastward and westward; for all the land which you see I will give to you and to your descendants forever. I will make your descendants [as numerous] as the dust of the earth, so that if a man could count the [grains of] dust of the earth, then your descendants could also be counted. Arise, walk (make a thorough reconnaissance) around in the land, through its length and its width, for I will give it to you" (Gen. 13:14-17).

God wanted Abram to act as though he already had the deed in his hand. God gave Abram a graphic picture of what it means to possess by faith what God had promised, even though it wouldn't be an actuality in Abram's lifetime.

> The Apostle Paul said this of believers:
> "By the word of truth, by the power of God; through weapons of righteousness for the right hand and the left, through glory and dishonor, through slander and good report; regarded as deceivers, yet true; as unknown, yet recognized; as dying, yet see—we live; as being disciplined, yet not killed; as grieving, yet always rejoicing; as poor, yet enriching many; as having nothing, yet possessing everything" (2 Corinthians 6:7-10).

In reading the story of Lot, we can see that there is much more to life than the outward and material. God spoke with Abram about what He wanted to give him because he had chosen to worship and follow after the Lord. Lot, however, was only given the choice to leave Sodom or perish with them. What a story of the contrast between following our heart into destruction or into blessing.

It's imperative we base our choices on God's Word, not on the assumptions of our culture. Those principles that God lays down encompass the whole Bible. While it takes a lifetime to learn them thoroughly, learn them we must.

CHOICE # 5
Choose to Allow Peace to be Your Umpire

"Let the peace of Christ [the inner calm of one who walks daily with Him] be the controlling factor [rule] in your hearts [deciding and settling questions that arise]. To this peace indeed you were called as members in one body [of believers]. And be thankful [to God always]" (Colossians 3:15).

As a believer, God's peace is always present in our heart to give us the direction we may so desperately need, but we might not always give it our permission to rule. Let's dig a little deeper into what this means. The understood subject of the first sentence of this passage is "you." *You* must let the peace of God rule in your heart.

The word "let" means "to give permission or opportunity to; allow" (American Heritage Dictionary).

The Greek word from which the word "rule" was translated is *brabeuo*, and it means "to arbitrate, to govern." (Strong's Concordance). Similarly, The Wuest translation of this phrase says, "Let the peace of God act as umpire in your heart." Just as every sport has disputes that must be settled by the officials, the peace of God is the umpire that settles all disputes as to what the will of God is for our lives. We must learn to listen to and heed the peace of God in our hearts just like an athlete defers to an umpire.

> **We can experience the God kind of peace that passes all understanding.**

Doesn't it make sense that God would put within His people the means to know what it is He wants us to do or the direction He wants us to travel? God's peace is something that every born-again believer has; it's a fruit of the Spirit (Gal. 5:22). That peace is always umpiring; we just don't always pay attention. How many times have we acted contrary to the peace in our hearts, and after we experienced failure we said, "I never did feel good about that." That was the peace of God umpiring, but we played by our own rules.

So what do we do when we don't sense peace in a direction we are headed and how do we facilitate the peace of God ruling? You may have heard the phrase, "mind the checks." In other words, when you get those inklings inside of yourself that something isn't right, don't just ignore them. Check them out and discern where they may be leading you or what choice they are trying to get you to make. Weigh your options, look for the decision that brings you the most peace, and trust God to guide you.

Recently, my wife and I had taken two weeks off to recharge our batteries, which included a trip to Colorado to visit some friends and take in a conference - one of our favorite things to do. Leading up to our departure date, I had this nagging feeling that I really didn't want to go, which was totally south of normal. On Sunday evening, a couple days before we were planning to leave, my wife agreed that we shouldn't go, which was *really* south of normal. In agreement, we postponed our trip and having made that decision, the peace came. Just an everyday decision, right?

Late that Sunday evening I began to experience chest pressure, which never got worse, but I knew was not normal. By mid-afternoon on Monday I called my doctor, but he was out of the office. I got an appointment for the next morning. About that same time the pressure in my chest stopped and never did return. I went to my scheduled appointment anyway the next morning, and when I told the doctor what happened the day before, he thought they should check it out. When the tests came back, He said either I'd had a heart attack and it was over, or I was on the verge of a big one. I was quickly sent by ambulance to the nearest heart hospital where a stent opened up a 99% blockage of the circumflex artery. Wow! Because they were able to treat me quickly, I have no heart damage and I'm doing great.

If we had continued the plan to leave for Colorado that day, who knows where or when the heart attack would have occurred? I listened to the unrest of my spirit not to go and drew confirmation from the peace that followed. Because of that one small decision, I avoided a potentially life-threatening consequence. Listening to the promptings of the Holy Spirit and responding to the peace that wants to umpire our decisions is absolutely necessary in making choices that lead to positive outcomes.

> Trust in and rely confidently on the LORD
> with all your heart and do not rely on your
> own insight or understanding. In all your

ways know and acknowledge and recognize Him, and He will make your paths straight and smooth [removing obstacles that block your way] (Prov. 3:5-6).

Another point to be made is that we must be moving for the Lord to steer us. The ship doesn't have to be going full steam ahead for the rudder to work, but it does have to be moving. Likewise, there will be times we have to act before the peace of God will give us perfect direction. We need to head where our heart is leading us and look for the peace.

We often hear the phrase, "wait upon the Lord" accompanied by teaching that we must sit and wait for God's direction. But when we are in a restaurant, does a waiter just come and stand by our table? No. They take our order and while the food is cooking they "wait" on other tables. Then they bring our food to us and go and "wait" some more, coming back to our table from time to time to see if we need anything. That's how we wait on the Lord; we make our requests known to Him, go about our business, and keep returning to His table to "wait" on him to see what He wants us to do.

Even if we make a mistake as we move forward with a decision, we will have made it in faith, trying to follow the peace of God in our hearts. The Lord can re-direct a wrong decision made in faith from a pure heart more than He can guide indecision.

What an awesome Father we have who literally has given us everything we need for life and godliness (2 Peter 1:3), including the peace-guided direction we need to make positive, everyday choices that can turn out to be monumental, life-changing opportunities. Praise His Name!

Here is another avenue of God that should be considered when we are looking for that supernatural peace to umpire our life: "Do not be anxious or worried about anything, but in everything [every circumstance and situation] by prayer and petition with thanksgiving, continue to make your [specific] requests known to God" (Phil. 4:6). This passage tells us not to be anxious or worried about anything. Tell me who in the world would think that is even possible? Most people are anxious and worried about *everything*.

In fact, anxiety disorders are the most common mental illness in the U.S., affecting 40 million adults in the United States age 18 and older – or 18.1% of the population every year. Antidepressant use among Americans is skyrocketing. Adults in the U.S. consumed four times more antidepressants in the late 2000s than they did in the early 1990s. As the third most frequently taken medication in the U.S., researchers estimate that eight to ten percent of the population is taking an antidepressant. (Anxiety and Depression Assn. of America [ADAA] 2018*)*

Many realize that anxiety and worry are not good and try to avoid them, yet do not believe that it is possible to live a life totally free of care. The Philippian passage above is just another part of the "peace*"* movement that God is interested in bestowing on His people. If we are operating in anxiety and worry, it impairs our ability to truly hear from God and make wise, godly decisions.

Paul commanded us to be anxious and worried for nothing.

How can we overcome anxiety and worry? First, we must come to fully believe God's Word is true and it will never change. We must believe Him when he says He will never leave us or forsakes us, that He will *always* meet our needs according to His riches in glory, that by His stripes we are healed. When those truths are the anchor in our decision making, we can relax in trusting that God's got our back.

Whether to be anxious and worried or calm and at peace is a choice determined by the filter we look through. Do we believe God and His Word, or do we believe we are victim to our circumstances? Scripture tells us to cast all our cares upon the Lord and when we do that with the full assurance of the truth of His Word, we have peace, even in the midst of tumultuous circumstances.

Paul commanded us to be anxious and worried for nothing. That means there is nothing that we should be anxious or worried about. There are no limits to the peace of God. The way we keep from being anxious and worried is to take our needs to the Lord in prayer and give thanks by faith that God has answered. Those who are still burdened have not totally cast their care over on to the Lord.

I experienced anxiety and unnatural fears that began in childhood and lasted into adulthood. It was only through knowing the Lord and the power of His Word that I was able to overcome those things. I realized through reading the Word that I didn't have to live with fear and anxiety. The Word of God is living, active, powerful and able to get into the depths of our being. The Word became a constant companion to me. I would quote it and declare it and most of all believe that it would work for me, and it did.

Perfect love casts out fear and there is no dread in God's kind of love (I John 4:18). The Word says we are to fear not, because God is with us. Take no thought for tomorrow, today has enough trouble of its own. I didn't have to worry about how long I had to deal with these things, only today. And little by little, reading, meditating, hearing and believing the truth over and over, I overcame.

Look at this encouragement from God: "...casting all your cares [all your anxieties, all your worries, and all your concerns, once and for all] on Him, for He cares about you [with deepest affection, and watches over you very carefully]" (1 Peter 5:7). What more assurance do we need? When we are able to cast our cares onto the Lord, an amazing thing happens, "...the peace of God [that peace which reassures the heart, that peace] which transcends all understanding, [that peace which] stands guard over your hearts and your minds in Christ Jesus [is yours]" (Phil. 4:7).

That peace is ours, already provided, already prepared for us, just waiting for us to trust God and His Word and it gets poured out and allows us to rest in Him. When we apply that to our decision-making process and ultimately the choices we make, it brings glory to the Lord and peace to us.

CHOICE # 6
Choose to Hear His Voice

C heck out this simple, but amazing verse of scripture found in John: "The sheep that are My own hear My voice and listen to Me; I know them, and they follow Me" (10:27). Jesus is not saying that believers *can* hear Him, or *could* hear Him, or *might* hear Him. He says if we are His sheep - believers in the Lord Jesus Christ - we *do* hear His voice and follow him. The word "hear" in this scripture happens both from the *logos* (written) Word of God and the *rhema* (spoken) Word of God, both vital in our decision-making processes. This is so important when trying to make everyday choices that can impact our life as well as for receiving healing and deliverance from the attacks of the enemy.

I read a book about a man who was a missionary overseas. After having been there for some time learning the language, he and his wife went out to a village to minister to the indigenous people where he contracted a serious disease. Doctors predicted the illness would cause him to be bedridden for at least four months.

Stuck flat on his back, this man began to remind God why he shouldn't be sick: he was a missionary, man of God, Bible college grad, following the call of God on his life, believed in healing, could *teach* healing. Yet somehow his personal achievements and holiness did nothing to change his situation. In desperation, he began to dig deeper. For the next four weeks he buried himself in reading the Word, listened to healing tapes, and read faith-filled books.

One morning, he awoke and shuffled out of his bedroom and was sitting alone. In the quiet, the Spirit of God spoke to him, "By My stripes you were healed." The missionary said he knew that scripture, he could teach that scripture, he wasn't a doubter of God's desire to heal him. But he said suddenly, what had been a doctrine BE-CAME LIFE! God spoke and he *knew* he was healed – so much so that he got dressed and walked down the street for the first time in weeks. From then on his body was quickly restored to full health; instead of four months in bed it was four weeks.

There are a number of critical points we can glean from this story. First, the Word of God spoken to the missionary that he was healed by Jesus' stripes (I Peter 2:24), didn't suddenly come alive that day it was revealed to him. It had always been alive! He had heard the verse before and even taught it, but had been living on auto-pilot and not creating for himself an environment to hear God. But when he really *heard* God, the verse became alive *within him* and he was healed. Hebrews tells us, "For the word of God is living and effective and sharper than any double-edged sword, penetrating as far as the separation of soul and spirit, joints and marrow. It is able to judge the thoughts and intentions of the heart" *(4:12)*.

This story also shows us that by spending that daily time *immersing* himself in the Word of God and focusing almost entirely on what God was saying, the missionary was creating an environment that enabled him to truly *hear* God. In spite of his calling, background and works for the Lord he'd done, hearing God wasn't an everyday priority. His time in bed gave him opportunity to eliminate distractions and focus on hearing God every day. Like the book of Matthew tells us, "It is written and forever remains written, 'Man shall not live by bread alone, but by every word that comes out of the mouth of God" (4:4).

Luke 5 also tells us, "But the news about Him was spreading farther, and large crowds kept gathering to hear Him and to be healed of their illnesses" (5:15). The news about Jesus spread and massive crowds continually gathered to *hear him speak* and to be healed from their illnesses. It was in the *hearing*, that they were able to receive *healing* from their illnesses.

Thirdly, the story of the missionary shows us that it is the *revelation* of an already known truth that brought faith and healing. The point is that just knowing about something, even knowing it well enough to teach it, isn't enough. TRUTH IS SPIRITUAL! Truth must be quickened to us in order for faith to be born and changes to occur. It isn't good enough just to *know* spiritual truth, it has to be *revealed* to us so it will manifest in our life.

When we are making choices that have the potential to really affect us and our loved ones, it is imperative to know that God's Word is living, active and powerful and wants to speak to us and give us direction. Listen to what Jesus said of the Jews of His day:

> Their minds are dull and slow to perceive, their ears are plugged and are hard of hearing, and they have deliberately shut their eyes to the truth. Otherwise they would open their eyes to see, and open their ears to hear, and open their minds to understand. Then they would turn to me and let me heal them (Matthew 13:15).

This passage shows that this condition of the heart is not something we are born with or that strikes us suddenly. It has to be nurtured over a prolonged period of time. This is the reason we should not violate our consciences, even in small things. This will keep us sensitive to God and will stop our hearts from becoming hardened to God.

When we harden ourselves to God and His Word, and then consequently cease to hear His voice, we begin making choices based on logic or wrong information which lead to less than positive outcomes. Spiritual ears

We must see ourselves as He sees us and to see Him as He really is.

become dull, vision becomes clouded. If our heart is out of tune with the Spirit of God it has difficulty *"hearing"* and faith is blocked. It's not doctrine or a belief system that should be relied upon to make godly choices, it is a fruit of *"hearing"* God. It will often be in our times of communion with the Father that His Word will be quickened to our spirits.

Hearing God, really hearing God (most often through His Word), is key to the healing of our bodies, to the deliverance of our infirmities, for the solution to our dilemmas, and the answers we are looking for to make good choices.

Unfortunately, many of us are afraid that if we stop to listen to God's voice, He will just pour down condemnation and judgement on us. In order for us to look forward to hearing His voice and receiving what He has to say, we must trust that He is a loving father and His Word is always for us and never against us. We must begin to see ourselves the way God sees us; not as failures, but as redeemed, as complete, as one with Him.

Early one morning I awoke and was spending time with the Lord. Instead of *choosing* to focus on God and His goodness and mercy that day, I *chose* to bemoan my failures and sins and was telling the Lord how sorry I was for them and asking Him to forgive me.

In that moment I saw a vision of a lake and saw myself standing on the shore of that lake. The lake was rather large with some trees on the shoreline. The lake was full of objects that looked like buoys bobbing on the waves. On each of those buoys was the name of sins.

I was then aware that Jesus was standing behind me and He said, "Those are your recent sins." I was absolutely appalled at the amount of my sins, but then the vision changed. I was standing on the shore of a vast ocean, looking at water as far as I could see. As with the lake, the ocean was full of buoys bobbing up and down, and each one of them had the name of sins. Jesus said, "Those are the sins of your lifetime." I put my head in my hands and fell to my knees in horror at the magnitude of it all.

When I looked up, all the names of my sins were gathering into a huge ball which Jesus took into His arms. Jesus drew His arm back like a discus thrower would and hurled the ball of my sin to the other side of the universe. Instantly this verse came to mind: "As far as the east is from the west, so far has He removed our transgressions from us" (Psalm 103:12).I once thought that meant from one side of the earth to the other, but the Lord showed me that when He casts our sins away from us, it's to the other side of the universe. What a powerful Truth the Lord gave me that day!

Since then I've lived with the assurance that God has done away with my sins, past, present and future so that I truly am the *righteousness of God in Christ Jesus.* Guilt and condemnation are no longer my companions and I trust Him to know He's not holding my sins to my account. It's truths like this that set us free to be what He wants us to be and the reason we must purpose to hear Him. He's gives us the *logos* word, the Bible, and He gives us His *rhema,* spoken word, so that we can know the Truth and the Truth will make and keep us free.

How often do we make choices and decisions while looking through the lens of sins, faults and failures instead of looking through the lens of God's forgiveness, grace and mercy. Looking through the filter of a sin-based conscience limits our possibilities and affects our ability to make profitable choices. God has forgiven us, cleansed us, made us righteous and calls us holy and blameless.

> He made Christ who knew no sin to [judi-
> cially] be sin on our behalf, so that in Him
> we would become the righteousness of

God [that is, we would be made acceptable to Him and placed in a right relationship with Him by His gracious lovingkindness] (2 Corinthians 5:21).

Is that how we look at ourselves? In order to truly make choices that bring about monumental outcomes, we must see ourselves as He sees us and to see Him as He really is.

In conclusion, *hearing* God is key to getting the best directions for our life. It is an amazing thing that we no longer must depend on our wisdom and understanding, but we have access to His. "In all your ways acknowledge Me and I will direct your steps" (Prov. 3:6) is a promise that gives us the assurance that our choices can be directed by God Himself. "Take my instruction rather than [seeking] silver, and take knowledge rather than choicest gold." (Prov. 8:10).Below is a list of Scriptures that can direct our steps as we seek to make choices:

For the LORD gives [skillful and godly] wisdom; from His mouth come knowledge and understanding (Prov. 2:6).

෴

The plans of the diligent lead surely to advantage, but everyone who is hasty comes surely to poverty (Prov. 21:5).

❧

Where there is no guidance the people fall, but in an abundance of counselors there is victory (Prov. 11:14).

❧

He who separates himself seeks his own desire. He quarrels against all sound wisdom (Prov. 18:1).

❧

A fool does not delight in understanding, but only in revealing his own mind (Prov. 18:2).

❧

The naïve believes everything, but the prudent man considers his steps (Prov. 14:15).

❧

A prudent man sees evil and hides himself, the naïve proceed and pay the penalty (Prov. 27:12).

CHOICE #7
Choose to Walk in Love

God tells us in His Word that He is Love (I John 4:8). He doesn't just operate in love, or loves at times, He *is* love. Love is the driving force behind all that He has done, all that He is and all that He will do. 1 Corinthians 13 tells us what love looks like:

> Love endures long and is patient and kind;
> love never is envious nor boils over with
> jealousy, is not boastful or vainglorious,
> does not display itself haughtily. It is not
> conceited (arrogant and inflated with

pride); it is not rude (unmannerly) and does not act unbecomingly. Love does not insist on its own rights or its own way, for it is not self-seeking; it is not touchy or fretful or resentful; it takes no account of the evil done to it [it pays no attention to a suffered wrong]. It does not rejoice at injustice and unrighteousness, but rejoices when right and truth prevail. Love bears up under anything and everything that comes, is ever ready to believe the best of every person, its hopes are fadeless under all circumstances, and it endures everything [without weakening]. Love never fails [never fades out or becomes obsolete or comes to an end]. Love never stops loving *(v. 4-8).*

Paul shared here the most detailed description of God's kind of love recorded in Scripture. He said what God's kind of love *is* (long-suffering, kind), and what it is *not* (envious, self-promoting, prideful). He demonstrates how God's love does *not* act (rudely, selfishly, easily provoked, does not think on evil, does not rejoice in unrighteousness),   and how it *does* act (rejoices

in truth, bears all things, believes all things, hopes all things, endures all things). He summed it all up in verse eight by saying that God's kind of love never stops loving.

These verses can be used as a checklist for us to see whether or not we are really operating in God's kind of love. Sometimes we think we have done everything possible, but have we really used God's kind of love? Here is a passage that tells us what the love of God does for us and how it helps us operate in Christ-likeness:

> Since we believe that Christ died for all of
> us, we should also believe that we have
> died to the old life we used to live. He died
> for all so that all who live–having received
> eternal life from him–might live no longer
> for themselves, to please themselves, but
> to spend their lives pleasing Christ who
> died and rose again for them (2 Cor. 5:14-
> 15 Living Bible).

Paul had just spoken of how some people considered him crazy because of the way he had neglected himself for the sake of others. Here, he gave the reason he lived that way. It was because the love of Christ dictated his life.

The love of God constrains us, compels us, motivates and empowers us to do the things that I've talked about in the previous chapters. When we know that Christ sacrificed Himself out of His love for us, we can believe what He says about us in His Word. We have literally died to our old self when we received Him as Savior. The old man is gone and the new man has come. The old ways, the doubts, the unbelief, the worry, anxiety, fretting, fear, lack of hope, poor choices etc. have been done away with through the shed blood of Christ.

We renew our minds daily to walk in God's kind of love.

We must renew our mind so that we believe and apply the new ways - His ways - to our lives. The new ways - faith, hope, trust, assurance and the ability to make good choices - have taken the "old self's" place. But we must renew our mind to that truth. We can now trust God to give us insight into our decision making and know with confidence that the choices we make are God's choices and will work to our good.

Watchman Nee, in his book *The Normal Christian Life*, gives us the perfect illustration when he states,

> You probably know the illustration of Fact, Faith and Experience walking along the top of a wall. Fact walked steadily on, turning neither to right nor left and never looking behind. Faith followed, and all went well so long as he kept his eyes focused upon Fact; but as soon as he became concerned about Experience and turned to see how he was getting on, he lost his balance and tumbled off the wall, and poor old Experience fell down after him. (2012, p. 43)

The temptation of the Christian life is to look only at the flesh, at ourselves and our experiences. The victory lies in looking away from self and unto Christ and the new creation facts. God's "divine power has given unto us all things that pertain unto life and godliness, through the knowledge of him" (2 Peter 1:3). That divine power is in

Him, and since He is in us, that divine power is within us as well.

It's no secret that we are no match for the devil, the flesh, and sin; but the devil, the flesh, and sin are no match for the living Christ who dwells within the believer. This truth comes through *knowledge* of Him, knowing Christ through His Word, believing it, receiving it and applying it to our life.

Here is why operating in God's kind of love is important in being able to make good choices so we have positive outcomes. God's type of love will never drive a person to behave improperly. Anyone who claims to be motivated by God's love and yet is acting contrary to God's Word is lying. God's Word and His love agree.

> **God's type of love is not an emotion. It is an act of the will.**

The world operates in an emotional love that overwhelms and often drives them to do acts that they don't want to do. For example, Hollywood has tried to convince us that love forces some people to commit adultery. They don't want to do it, but they "fall in love" and can't control themselves.

God's kind of love is not that way. God's type of love often *involves* emotions, but it is *not* an emotion. It is an act of the will. We can choose to love even when we don't feel like it. We can always conduct ourselves in a godly manner. We can make choices that bless ourselves and others. Paul told Titus to have the older women in the church at Crete teach the younger women to love their husbands and their children (Titus 2:4). What a radical concept. Most believe that people fall in love and out of love, but they can't choose to love; it's either there or it's not. However, God's kind of love is a choice. Jesus didn't feel some emotional sensation when He chose to die for us, but that was the greatest demonstration of God's kind of love that the world has ever seen. He made a choice in spite of His emotions.

"Now My soul is troubled and deeply distressed; what shall I say? 'Father, save Me from this hour [of trial and agony]'? But it is for this[very] purpose that I have come to this hour [this time and place]." John 12:27. Because He was consumed with His Father's love, Jesus acted properly, even when His emotions didn't agree. We know what the outcome of that was ...MONUMENTAL!

1 Corinthians 13:5 tells us that God's kind of love is not self-seeking. *Agape* love will cause people to lay

down their lives for others (John 15:13), because they have literally forgotten themselves. Often, when heroes are asked why they chose to put themselves in jeopardy to save someone else, they reply that they didn't even think about themselves; all they thought of was the danger to the other person. That's God's kind of love.

Therefore, God's kind of love is the antidote to selfishness and pride. We cannot conquer self by focusing on self. The only way to win over self is to fall in love with God more than with ourselves. It is in discovering God's love that we lose self-love. Operating in God's kind of love will cause us to do the right thing; to make choices that are biblically based and hence will produce positive outcomes.

When people are walking in God's kind of love, they are easy to get along with, they don't have "short fuses" and operate in anger. God's kind of love does not carry a chip on its shoulder. God's kind of love is positive. God's kind of love focuses on the good things in others and in situations.

Paul said: "but I want you to be wise in what is good and innocent in what is evil (Romans 16:19(b)). Here's what God's kind of love thinks upon:

Whatever is true, whatever is honorable and worthy of respect, whatever is right and confirmed by God's word, whatever is pure and wholesome, whatever is lovely and brings peace, whatever is admirable and of good repute; if there is any excellence, if there is anything worthy of praise, think continually on these things [center your mind on them, and implant them in your heart] (Phil. 4:8).

Paul was telling the Philippian believers to reflect and meditate upon positive principles of thinking that would lead to victorious Christian living. In the Greek, what Paul is saying is constructed in the present imperative, which is a command to do something in the future that involves a continuous and repeated action. Paul is telling us to think on and practice these things *constantly* for the remainder of our lives and they will produce the positive outcomes that God wants us to have.

> **Truth is truth whether we are at church, at home, or on the jobsite.**

Did you notice Paul's use of the word "whatever"? There are many who think this verse can only be fulfilled by thinking on "church" things or "religious" things. Paul, however, said "whatever" falls into the following categories: (true, honorable, worthy of respect, right, confirmed by God's word, pure and wholesome, lovely and brings peace, admirable, of good repute.) Therefore, it is not only thinking about *spiritual* truths that is important; we also need to be able to discern natural truths from lies and think on those things, too.

In fact, our lives should not necessarily be compartmentalized into "spiritual" and "secular." Truth is truth whether we are at church or at home or on the jobsite. We should keep our minds stayed on the good things God has given us in the natural such as family, health, and work, just as we should think about righteousness, justification, forgiveness, etc.

We will seldom do anything that we have not thought about first. So, Paul is telling us to *think* on those things that will positively influence our actions and choices so we have beneficial outcomes. We must come to know the love of God and the truth of His Word; which is the sole source of right thinking that brings victory to every area of our lives.

The love of God helps us to forget the past because God tells us in His Word that He has forgotten our past. We know by His Word that we have been given His authority and can trample on the deceits and obstacles thrown at us by the devil. The love of God gives us His supernatural peace that passes understanding. The love of God keeps our hearts and minds calm even under stress. The love of God gives us what we need to make choices that lead to monumental outcomes of the blessed kind; outcomes that God has ordained for us through His Son Jesus Christ.

CHOICE # 8
Choose Those Things of Eternal Value

Jesus, of course, is the prime example of One who was faced with choices daily, yet the Bible says He was without sin. In other words, Jesus always made good choices that had eternal value.

There are those who would say, "of course Jesus didn't sin and always made the right choices because He was God." The Bible tells us that Jesus laid down His divinity and became fully man. Jesus had to face everyday choices continually, just like we do. The only difference is the outcome of His decisions affected the entirety of His Creation.

See the pattern of His decisions from day one of

His ministry,

> After Jesus was baptized, He came up im-
> mediately out of the water; and behold, the
> heavens were opened, and he (John) saw
> the Spirit of God descending as a dove and
> lighting on Him (Jesus), and behold, a
> voice from heaven said, "This is My be-
> loved Son, in whom I am well-pleased and
> delighted (Matthew 3:16-17)!

How amazing is this! Go into the waters of baptism and come out with the God of the heavens speaking audibly about how great you are. Talk about an opportunity for an ego trip! Jesus could have launched from there, "Hey did you all hear that? Get over here and worship Me!" But instead, the Bible tells us that Jesus left

Jesus had to face everyday choices continually, just like we do.

the awe of the crowds and was led into the wilderness to be tempted by the devil.

When Jesus came out of the wilderness after 40 days of fasting, the devil was right there to offer Him a solution for His hunger. He then offered him a chance to prove His invincibility by jumping off a building because the angels would catch Him. Finally Jesus was offered all the land He could see (which the devil had a right to offer him), if He would only bow down and worship him. Each temptation offered a choice. Say yes or say no, yet the consequences would be monumental.

Throughout the rest of His ministry, Jesus had to continually make many of the same everyday choices that we have to make; whether to follow His own path or make choices based on the will of His heavenly Father.

In Luke, we see Jesus' heart-wrenching choice whether to follow His own feelings or choose God's plan, "And He withdrew from them about a stone's throw, and knelt down and prayed, saying, "Father, if You are willing, remove this cup [of divine wrath] from Me; yet not My will, but [always] Yours be done" (Luke 22:41-42).

In this same way, we should live our lives: "Lord here's an idea I have, a choice I have to make, a direction I want to take, but Lord, in everything, your will be done. Lord, I want your desires above my desires because I know you have my best interest in mind and your way is always better than my way."

The story of Joseph is another good example of a young man who made good, eternal choices in the face of adversity that had monumental impact. As a young man, he was the favorite of his father but absolutely hated by his ten older brothers. His brothers eventually got so jealous of his self-confidence and favor with their dad that they beat him up, threw him down a well, sold him to human traffickers, and told their father he was dead. Made a slave, thrown in prison to rot, forgotten, wrongly accused, and rejected by his own family, this young man had many opportunities to be bitter, resentful,

> **I would rather live my life believing there is a God and in the end find out there isn't, than live my life believing there isn't a God and finding out there is.**
> -unknown

and resign himself to the unfairness of his circumstances. If he had, he may have died a slave in a dank prison cell; an unknown man of no consequence.

Instead, whatever situation he was in he chose to have a positive attitude, look for ways to serve, and do things God's way. Joseph's daily choices ultimately spared the entire nation of Egypt during drought. His choices kept his family from starvation and saved what we now know to be the very bloodline of Jesus Christ.

Like Joseph, when we face difficult decisions we first take God into account and make those choices in line with *His* promises and principles, not the immediate gratification of the flesh. We have to trust that when we deny ungodliness and worldly desires, there is an eternal outcome and an eternal reward.

Unfortunately, many in the world and even in the church world want to seek other things first and add the kingdom of God later. Sometimes the later never comes. Instead, to make choices of eternal value, we must "Seek first the kingdom of God and His righteousness and all these things will be added to you" (Matthew 6:33).

Following are three strategies you can use as a guide for making right choices on things of eternal value that produce monumental outcomes:

1. MAKE CHOICES WHICH VALUE RELATIONSHIPS OVER HAVING OUR OWN WAY

Strife could be avoided in the family and in the church if we would lay down our rights and instead, put a premium on our relationships. The next time you are about to quarrel with someone (and quarrelling is a choice we make!), stop and think about whether the quarrel is rooted in godly principle or in selfishness. Sometimes we need to confront sin or take a stand for the truth, even though it causes conflict. Be careful! It's easy to justify selfishness by calling it righteous anger. Here is a good rule of thumb in choosing relationship over rights, "So then, let us pursue [with enthusiasm] the things which make for peace and the building up of one another [things which lead to spiritual growth]" (Romans 14:19).

2. MAKE CHOICES WHICH VALUE GODLINESS OVER OUR DESIRE FOR THINGS.

The Scriptures tell us that by faith Abram had already renounced everything visible and opted for the unseen promises of God. He had no need. Lot, on the other hand, lifted up his eyes and chose the land which looked the best to him. Lot chose by sight and ended up completely bankrupt. He escaped Sodom with seemingly nothing and spent the rest of his life living in a cave. The things he saw and eventually gained, didn't bring him the lasting happiness he expected. Abram chose by faith, not by sight, and ended up spiritually and financially blessed, seeing and possessing by faith the whole land of Canaan. Lot lived for greed and came up empty. Abram lived for God and came up full.

How can we know whether we are under the influence of greed? I read this account by a man named Charles Simeon, a godly 19th century British pastor who offered three criteria for evaluating ourselves. (*Expository Outlines on the Whole Bible* [Zondervan], XII:469-471):

First, we may judge ourselves by the manner in which we *seek* the things of this world. If we find ourselves thinking more about the things of this world and how to get them than about God; or if the thought of having them brings us more pleasure than our thoughts about God; or if we are willing to violate our conscience or neglect spiritual duties to pursue those things, then we are governed by greed.

Second, we may judge ourselves by the manner in which we *enjoy* the things of this world. There is nothing wrong with enjoying the things God provides us. However, if we start thinking, "If I just had such and such, I would be happy." If we think that by getting so much in the bank, we will be secure from the trials of life, then we've shifted our trust from God to material things, and we are governed by greed.

Third, we may judge ourselves by the manner in which we *mourn the loss* of the things of this world. Paul claimed to be content with much or with little, because Christ was his sufficiency. If our joy is dependent on our possessions or if we are filled with anxiety and grief if we lose them, then we are more governed by greed than by God.

What is the answer when we ask the question, *What are we really living for?* If it's Christ and His kingdom, "the things of earth grow strangely dim, in the light of His glory and grace," as the song goes.

3. MAKE CHOICES WHICH VALUE FELLOWSHIP WITH GOD OVER WHAT THE WORLD OFFERS.

"For what does it benefit a man to gain the whole world [with all its pleasures], and forfeit his soul" (Mark 8:36)? Why is it easier to operate carnally that it is to operate spiritually? The reason is we live in the physical; we see, we hear, we experience. Our focus is on our five senses and we put more stock in that than we do in the things we cannot see.

Here is how God sees it: "So we look not at the things which are seen, but at the things which are unseen; for the things which are visible are temporal [brief and fleeting], but the things which are invisible are everlasting and imperishable" (2 Cor. 4:18).

When we read of Paul's life, he reduced the impact of his afflictions by remembering that everything he suffered in this life was "but for a moment." In this verse, Paul made it very clear how he accomplished this. He focused

> **Our emotions and attitudes follow what we think.**

his attention on the invisible truths of the spiritual realm, which were eternal, instead of the visible things of this physical world, which are all passing away.

Our emotions and attitudes follow what we think. Are we thinking on the things of God which are eternal, or on our everyday that's fleeting? Here's how Mark described how we miss the things of God if we aren't purposefully looking for them:

> Then He got into the boat with them, and the wind ceased; and they were completely overwhelmed, because they had not understood [the miracle of] the loaves [how it revealed the power and deity of Jesus]; but [in fact] their heart was hardened [being oblivious and indifferent to His amazing works] (Mark 6:51-52).

The disciples were, by all accounts, in fellowship with Jesus. Yet they missed the significance of what He was doing because they failed to understand. I pray quite often; "Lord let me see how You see and hear how you hear."

When we focus our attention on our problems, they get magnified out of proportion. When we neglect our problems and think on God's provision, the answer gets magnified and the problem shrinks. Whatever we think upon is going to dominate us. If we think on depressing things, we'll be depressed. If we think on uplifting things, we'll be uplifted. If we think "By His stripes, we were healed," we'll be healed. If our thinking is sick, we'll be sick. The battle is for our minds.

The word "temporal" (2 Cor. 4:18) means temporary. Any problem that we can see is limited by time. It will pass. However, spiritual truths, including our union with Christ and all the benefits that entails, are forever. When problems begin to oppress us, we should tell them that they're only temporary and look to the eternal promises of God. Choose those things that are of lasting value. Value the fellowship with God and all that includes rather than yearning for the offerings of the world.

FINAL THOUGHTS

Choices; we may not always enjoy them, but we are stuck with them. We may run from them, but they will always be there waiting when we stop. The key is facing our options and making good choices. We must choose to make choices based on God's principles: Relationships over rights; godliness over greed; fellowship with God over the world's approval; faith in God's promises over immediate pleasure from the world. If we have God and His promises, we have everything we need to make positive, life giving choices that will enhance our life and not destroy it.

In our world today, we have available to us more books, articles and "how-to" manuals, websites and internet postings than we can read in a lifetime. A myriad of resources give us directions on how to live, what products to use, what kind of relationships to have, and what *they* have done to make their life wonderful. Most are probably well meaning and perhaps even helpful. Every day, however, we need a foundation of hope and balance that will take us through our life with the minimum of strife, heartache and trouble. That is found in the blessed Word of God. Do we recognize that God does have an advantage in knowing what is good for us and what decisions we should make?

> Trust in and rely confidently on the LORD
> with all your heart and do not rely on your
> own insight or understanding. In all your
> ways know and acknowledge and recognize Him, And He will make your paths
> straight and smooth [removing obstacles
> that block your way] (Prov. 3:5-6).

What a loving Savior we have; one who went to the cross without a guarantee that any of His creation would recognize what He had done for them or would ever surrender their hearts to Him! He promises to always be with those who do come to Him. He promises to give them wisdom to make good choices in their life and be a witness and testimony to the greatness of God.

This final passage of scripture best explains what making good, positive choices under His direction accomplishes:

> For we are His workmanship [His
> own master work, a work of art], created

in Christ Jesus [reborn from above—spiritually transformed, renewed, ready to be used] for good works, which God prepared [for us] beforehand [taking paths which He set], so that we would walk in them [living the good life which He prearranged and made ready for us] (Eph. 2:10).

We have a choice, a free will, to choose to follow God as Lord of our life or to live under the renegade power of the devil. That's the only two spiritual choices we have on the earth and the choices we make will dictate our life into eternity. Every day of our life we are faced with choices, and some of those will have monumental outcomes. Choose wisely!

*   *   *

Made in the USA
Columbia, SC
11 March 2019